First World War
and Army of Occupation
War Diary
France, Belgium and Germany

41 DIVISION
Divisional Troops
189 and 190 Brigade Royal Field Artillery
3 May 1916 - 30 April 1917

WO95/2625/3

The Naval & Military Press Ltd
www.nmarchive.com
Published in association with The National Archives

Published by

The Naval & Military Press Ltd

Unit 10 Ridgewood Industrial Park,

Uckfield, East Sussex,

TN22 5QE England

Tel: +44 (0) 1825 749494

www.naval-military-press.com

www.nmarchive.com

This diary has been reprinted in facsimile from the original. Any imperfections are inevitably reproduced and the quality may fall short of modern type and cartographic standards.

© **Crown Copyright**
Images reproduced by permission of The National Archives, London, England, 2015.

Contents

Document type	Place/Title	Date From	Date To
Heading	WO95/2625/4 41 Div 189 Bde RFA May 16-Apr 17		
Heading	41st Division 189th Brigade R.F.A. May 1916-Apr 1917 To 1 Army		
Heading	War Diary Of 189th Brigade RFA. From 3rd May 1916 To 31st May 1916 Vol. I 189 RFA Vol 1		
War Diary	N. Camp Aldershot	03/05/1916	03/05/1916
War Diary	Havre	04/05/1916	05/05/1916
War Diary	Hazebrouck	06/05/1916	27/05/1916
War Diary	No. Of Armentieres	27/05/1916	31/05/1916
Map	Sketch Map. I.		
War Diary	Maction No Armentieres.	01/06/1916	21/08/1916
War Diary	Eecke	22/08/1916	24/08/1916
War Diary	Cocquerel	25/08/1916	01/09/1916
War Diary	Argoeuves	02/09/1916	02/09/1916
War Diary	Dernancourt	03/09/1916	05/09/1916
War Diary	Bazentin Le Grand	06/09/1916	17/09/1916
War Diary	H.Q. 1000 N Of Longueval	18/09/1916	19/09/1916
War Diary	1000 XW Of Longueval	20/09/1916	24/09/1916
War Diary	H.Q. 1000 XW Of Longueval	25/09/1916	30/09/1916
Operation(al) Order(s)	Artillery 41st Divisional Order No. 14	16/09/1916	16/09/1916
Operation(al) Order(s)	1st Divisional Artillery Order No. 10	14/09/1916	14/09/1916
Miscellaneous	Amendment to 41st Divl. Artillery Order No. 10	14/09/1916	14/09/1916
Operation(al) Order(s)	41st Division Artillery Order No. 16	17/09/1916	17/09/1916
War Diary	HQ. 1000 X W. Of Longueval	01/10/1916	31/10/1916
War Diary	Montauban	01/11/1916	01/11/1916
War Diary	Laneuville	02/11/1916	03/11/1916
War Diary	Talmas	04/11/1916	04/11/1916
War Diary	Amplier	05/11/1916	05/11/1916
War Diary	Boubers	06/11/1916	06/11/1916
War Diary	Heuchin	07/11/1916	09/11/1916
War Diary	Berguette	10/11/1916	10/11/1916
War Diary	Wallon-Cappel	11/11/1916	11/11/1916
War Diary	Godwaersvelde	12/11/1916	12/11/1916
War Diary	H.Q. 500 Yards N.E. Of Dicke Busche	13/11/1916	30/11/1916
Miscellaneous	Officers Commanding.	26/11/1916	26/11/1916
Operation(al) Order(s)	41st Divisional Artillery Operation Order No. 42		
Miscellaneous	Schedule "A"		
Miscellaneous	Schedule B		
War Diary	H.Q. 500 Yds NE Of Dicke Busche	01/12/1916	02/12/1916
War Diary	HQ 400 Yds N. Of Dicke Busche	03/12/1916	31/12/1916
War Diary	H.Q. 500 Yards N Of Dickebusch	01/01/1917	12/01/1917
War Diary	HQ At La Clytte	13/01/1917	31/01/1917
War Diary	La Clytte	13/02/1917	13/02/1917
War Diary	La Clytte Of Dickebusche	14/02/1917	27/02/1917
War Diary	H.Q. Dickebusche	28/02/1917	28/02/1917
War Diary	H.Q. 500 Yds NE Of Dickebusche	01/03/1917	12/03/1917
War Diary	Dickebusche	13/03/1917	16/03/1917
War Diary	Houtkerque	17/03/1917	18/03/1917
War Diary	Riveldt.	19/03/1917	20/03/1917
War Diary	Noordpeene	21/03/1917	21/03/1917

War Diary	Muircque Nicurllet	22/03/1917	31/03/1917
War Diary	Muncq Nieurlet	01/04/1917	07/04/1917
War Diary	Noordpeene	08/04/1917	08/04/1917
War Diary	Renninghelst	09/04/1917	19/04/1917
War Diary	Ypres	20/04/1917	30/04/1917

WO 95/2625/4
B 41 DIV
189 BDE RFA May '16 -
Capt '17

41ST DIVISION

189TH BRIGADE R.F.A.
MAY 1916 - APR 1917.

To I ARMY

original

CONFIDENTIAL.

WAR DIARY
OF
189ᵗʰ BRIGADE RFA.
from 3ʳᵈ May 1916 to 31ˢᵗ May 1916.
Vol. I.

SECRET.

189. Bde R.F.A. page 1

Army Form C. 2118.

WAR DIARY
or
INTELLIGENCE SUMMARY.
(Erase heading not required.)

Instructions regarding War Diaries and Intelligence Summaries are contained in F. S. Regs., Part II. and the Staff Manual respectively. Title pages will be prepared in manuscript.

Place	Date	Hour	Summary of Events and Information	Remarks and references to Appendices
N. Camp Aldershot	1916. 3rd/5		Brigade left from Gov. Siding Aldershot in 11 trains. 1st train leaving 6.50 AM last 3.20 P.M. arrived at SOUTHAMPTON DOCKS 9.5 A.M. — 5.30 P.M. Embarkation 4 different ships. Sailed early in morning of 4th may having been delayed by fog in starting.	
HAVRE	4/5		Arrived during the afternoon. Camped for the night.	
"	5/5		Entrained in 5 trains starting throughout the day.	
HAZEBROUCK	6/5		Arrived during the day having detrained at STEENBECQUE Stn.	
	9/5		Went into billets in farms 1 & 2 miles N.E. of HAZEBROUCK. A portion of Bde moved out to the positions occupied by 5th Bde R.F.A. 9th Divn North of ARMENTIERES for instructional purposes.	
	17/5		Above mentioned returned to HAZEBROUCK being replaced by rest of Bde.	
	22/5		The Brigade Ammunition Column was broken up portion being sent to D.A.C. & a portion to Trench Mortars.	
	27/5		The Bde HQ & portion in rear moved up to the position of 57th Bde R.F.A. HQ & Bty, taking over from that Bde which moved back to HAZEBROUCK. 12 hrs From this hour D/189 became A/183 Bde. A/183 (Howitzer Bty) becoming D/189.	(see sketch I)

WAR DIARY or INTELLIGENCE SUMMARY.

Army Form C. 2118.

189 Bde RFA.   page 2.

Place	Date	Hour	Summary of Events and Information	Remarks and references to Appendices
N. of ARMENTIERES.	1916 27/5		The 4 M.G. of 189 & A/85/183. occupy positions covering Right sector & that is at present held by 9 Bn. These M.G. constitute the Right group. No retaliatory action took place after taking over. Enemy fired a few rounds checking registing & shelling and by way of retaliation. South African Bde of infty occupy trenches in this section.	Weather fine sunny.
	28/5		"	
	29/5		"	
	30.5.		"	
	31/5		Handed over to 122 Inf Bde. 41st Division, consisting of 20 Durham L.I., 10 R.W.Kent, 11 Queens, 23 Middlesex. W. McClintock Comdg 189 Bde RFA	

31/5/16. W. McClintock
Comdg 189 Bde RFA

WAR DIARY
INTELLIGENCE SUMMARY. 169 Bde RFA.

Page 3. Vol 2.

Army Form C. 2118.

Place	Date	Hour	Summary of Events and Information	Remarks and references to Appendices
In action Nr ARMENTIERES.	1916 1/6	1.30	C/169 Took on an enemy M.G. with aeroplane observation. There were 6 enemy balloons up at time. About 2.30 p.m. enemy began shelling A/183 about 100. 5.9" H.E. were fired – per front detachments had been withdrawn so there were no casualties. Gun had a wheel & sights damaged. Bdy horse lines were evacuated after dark. #2 guns moved to a prepared posn at C.14.C.8.9. Gun remained in detached posn on left of former posn.	hyme
	2.6.		Normal artillery action on both sides.	hyme
	3.6.		ditto.	weather fine
	4.6.		ditto. 3rd gun of A/183. moved to C.14.C.8.9.	hyme
	5/6.		A very quiet day. High wind S.W. showery.	hyme
	6/6		Normal artillery fire on both sides.	hyme

WAR DIARY or INTELLIGENCE SUMMARY. 189" Bde. CFA.

Army Form C. 2118.

page 4.

Place	Date	Hour	Summary of Events and Information	Remarks and references to Appendices
In action N of ARMENTIERES.	7/6.		Normal activity.	
	8/6.	3 p.m.	Prearranged Bombardment of enemy line in V.28. began. Following units of the Bde. took part, ammn. expended :- B/189. fired 160 rds at enemy trenches 3.10 - 3.45 p.m. 2 Hows. g D/189. fired 60 rounds at V.28.a.4.6. 3.15 - 3.45 " C/189. 1 gun fired 30 rds at V.29.d.9½.7½. 3.10 - 3.45 " " " " " V.29.c.3.3 " The result was said to be satisfactory. Enemy retaliated.	hper
	9/6.		Enemy continued retaliation by shelling heavily certain of our trenches & OPs. We replied.	hper
	10/6.		Enemy shelled LE TOUQUET Stn. heavily. C.9.d.5.4. damaging C/189. O.P. Casualties 1 man slightly wounded B/189	hper
	11/6.		A quiet day. High west wind. Rain.	hper

WAR DIARY
or
INTELLIGENCE SUMMARY. 189th Bde RFA.

Army Form C. 2118.

Page 5

Place	Date	Hour	Summary of Events and Information	Remarks and references to Appendices
In action N. of ARMENTIERES	13/6		Little activity on either side. Weather cold, wet, windy NW & W.	4/pr R.
	14/6		ditto. ditto.	
	15/6		ditto. ditto.	
	16/6	Am 11.15	Enemy t[rench] dug's had warning "Gas Alert" from before M.N. "Gas alarm" went. All precautions taken, men wore [anti-gas] helmets. Gas cloud which had been discharged somewhere about MESSINES passed us by & the westward. Razor wire South of NIEPPE for a little ½ in.	
	17/6		normal. Fine. Wind N. NE.	4/pr R.
	18/6	PM 11.45	ground during day. Many enemy batterys up. Clear fire Gas alarm. 2 cylinders of gas opened (or wind N. NE.)	
20th normal	20/6		Gas worn left. Didn't get here on way. Plans by Ctl L 1.30 pm before D/189. Shelled German Machine Gun home "heavily," repaid much damage (C.10.6.56)	
	21/6		done. This annoyed enemy who retaliated & shelled OP's at C.9 d 5.4. before Enemy retaliated on various points	

Army Form C. 2118.

WAR DIARY or INTELLIGENCE SUMMARY.

189th Bde RFA. page 6.

(Erase heading not required.)

Instructions regarding War Diaries and Intelligence Summaries are contained in F. S. Regs., Part II. and the Staff Manual respectively. Title pages will be prepared in manuscript.

Place	Date	Hour	Summary of Events and Information	Remarks and references to Appendices
In action N of ARMENTIERES	22/6		Normal activity.	
	23/6		ditto. About MN. fairly heavy gas.	
	24/6	(9pm about)	Enemy shelled our trenches about C4C 9.6 very heavily and knocked them about considerably. They were supported by 10" R" What Ken K.A. A.A.	
		PM 9-10-20	Time. B/189 & A/183 replied by shelling the enemy trenches opposite. Considerable damage was reported. 3.61 rounds expended.	Casualties A/189. 1 man slight wounded C4C 9.8 & C4C 9.6
		20/75	Enemy artillery activity about the conclusion of the Div. Mine Bty series enemy began shelling them evidently having located them by their flash. 6 L.G. rounds were fired at each Bty and then enemy fire ceased. were and did nothing & green to jump from shell hole otherwise. 4.2" or 5.9".	Fair. Wind W. mur.
	25/6		Normal activity.	Casualties D/189. 1 man wounded weather light Fair. Wind W.
	26/6		" "	" " mur.

WAR DIARY
or
INTELLIGENCE SUMMARY. 189th Bde RFA. page 7.
(Erase heading not required.)

Army Form C. 2118.

Place	Date	Hour	Summary of Events and Information	Remarks and references to Appendices
N.W. ARMENTIERES. 27.6.16.			Normal activity.	Some rain. Wind W.
	28.		"	Some rain. Wind W.
	29.		"	" " "
	30.	7pm.	In accordance with scheme for raiding enemys trenches 2 guns A/183 & 4 guns B/189 started to cut the enemys wire at C10b40-C4a75.3.-C4a7.5. 2 guns A/183 were to "pretend" to cut wire at C4c9.8-C4c8.9%. A/189 also has employed on a similar mission from C4a 5.2 to C4a 2 4t. C/189. Wire trees off to deal with any O.P's & enemy wire likely to annoy D/189. Wire trees off for Counter Bty work. B/189. # Task was completed on "factory" wire about 380 rds. The two guns A/183 were not so successful. The wire they cut stands with wire not in the actual spot wished by the infantry & the open they did wish cut was in a slight hollow & the task was not completed.	
		9.15 pm.	Batteries bombarded front line trenches till 9.45 PM when they ceased fire	

Army Form C. 2118.

WAR DIARY
or
INTELLIGENCE SUMMARY. 189th Bde R.F.A. page 8.
(Erase heading not required.)

Instructions regarding War Diaries and Intelligence Summaries are contained in F.S. Regs., Part II. and the Staff Manual respectively. Title pages will be prepared in manuscript.

Place	Date	Hour	Summary of Events and Information	Remarks and references to Appendices
N. of ARMENTIERES	30/6	P.M. 10.0	Gas & smoke let off from our trenches	
		10.0½	Bombardment restarted & continued till 10.28, when rifles lifted their fire & barraged till 10.53 when they ceased. At 10.28½ the Infy advanced. Several small raiding parties opposite points where wire had been supposed to be cut. The party on right found the wire at C.10 d 4.4 uncut & the parapet manned by Germans, so it retired. On app. C 4 a 7.3 - C 4 a 7.5, party got through but found trenches deserted. W.P.R.	

W.M.Cecil T.R.C.
O.C. 189 Bde R.F.A.

41/

Army Form C. 2118.

WAR DIARY
or
INTELLIGENCE SUMMARY. 189 Bde RFA. July page (1)
(Erase heading not required.)

Vol 3

Instructions regarding War Diaries and Intelligence Summaries are contained in F. S. Regs., Part II. and the Staff Manual respectively. Title pages will be prepared in manuscript.

Place	Date	Hour	Summary of Events and Information	Remarks and references to Appendices
N of ARMENTIERES.	1916 July 1st		Normal activity. Fine weather.	
"	2nd		A quiet day till 7.45 P.M. when according to orders Bdys started shelling enemy's communications in rear. He retaliated on our trenches and the infantry asked for retaliation. This was kept going until about 10.30 P.M. A/183 & B/189. shelling enemy's support trenches. D/189. engaging enemy Bdys as far as they could be located. C/189 retaliated on captured HQ & 18". in front of trenches being shelled. B/189 was shelled about 9 P.M by 5.9 & 4.2. No 2 gun emplacement was hit at the back. No no.1 was killed & 3 men wounded.	
		10.10 P.M.	According to arrangement 2 Guns B/189. C/189. A/189 D/189. shelled enemy trenches East of ARMENTIERES to assist New Zealand Div who were carrying out raid. Casualties 1 killed 3 wounded	
		12 N		weather fine, wind N. W. breeze

T.134. Wt. W708—776. 500000. 4/15. Sir J. C. & S.

Army Form C. 2118.

WAR DIARY
or
INTELLIGENCE SUMMARY. 189 Bde R.F.A.   July 1916 [2]
(Erase heading not required.)

Instructions regarding War Diaries and Intelligence Summaries are contained in F.S. Regs., Part II. and the Staff Manual respectively. Title pages will be prepared in manuscript.

Place	Date	Hour	Summary of Events and Information	Remarks and references to Appendices
N of ARMENTIERES	1916. July 3.		A quiet day.	
	4.		ditto.	appx
	5.		"	
	6.		"	appx
	7.		"	
	8.		"	appx
	9.	8.30 am	D/189. shelled by 5.9" from 8.30 am till about 12.30 pm. about 150 rounds fell in vicinity of guns. no damage done except 1 S.M. wounded. 7 hostile balloons were visible throughout the day. also his aeroplanes very active all day.	
		8 pm	30 rounds fired into LE BISET.	
			very fine day. kind W.	appx
			Cancelled / wounded	
	10.		A quiet day	
	11.		"	hours

Army Form C. 2118.

WAR DIARY
or
INTELLIGENCE SUMMARY.

189 Bde RFA.
July page 3

(Erase heading not required.)

Place	Date	Hour	Summary of Events and Information	Remarks and references to Appendices
No 2 ARMENTIERES	12.	8 AM	A/183 started L cut wire at Nor C 4 d 4 2 i. with a view to raid at night. B 15/189 was to demonstrate a wire cut at U 28 a 6 3 & C/189 at LE TOUQUET Salient, but owing to report from F.O.O. that he had heard (telephonic) discussing the operation on the wire operation postponed. Wire cutting operations suspended at 11.30 AM. A/183 who had moved over 2 of their guns for the operation from C14 a 90 to C8 C6 2 were ordered there & half 1 man wounded. Casualties A/183 1 man wounded.	Weather dull & light showers. Wind S.
	13.	8 AM	Wire cutting again started. But owing L. Captn. of one of our inf. on patrol, it was decided to abandon contemplated raid. Wire cutting however had to go on & in place of raid, bursts of fire from all the Batteries were to be delivered on the front line & support trenches in vicinity of where the wire had been cut in hopes of getting some of the enemy prepared to meet the raid. In addition hits Aim ockwm? thus from 3' bursts of fire were delivered at 10.31, 10.46, 10.58. A/183 was again ordered at C8 C6 2 but had no casualties.	LMcN

WAR DIARY or INTELLIGENCE SUMMARY.

Army Form C. 2118.

189 Bde RFA July page 4.

Place	Date	Hour	Summary of Events and Information	Remarks and references to Appendices
N of ARMENTIERES	14/7		A quiet day.	
	15/7		LE BIZET shelled from 8 A.M - 1.30 P.M with 5.9" & 77 m/m also from 3 P.M 5 - 3.30. 3 how rounds HE 8 7/8 gun 3/4 87 rounds. 5 or 6 shots at 12 noon to turn 3 1/5 on L line cut ar C 4 d 2.0 - c4b.15. A/189. 3. B/189. C/189 were employed in wire all afternoon.	Casualties A/189. 3 men wounded B/189 2 men D/189 4 men
	16/7		Continued wire cutting as above. at 9.15 & 10.11 shelled LES ECLUSES & PONT ROUGE. accordg to SAM Rd D'd' Order. Enemy retaliation slight.	dull cloudy win W.
	17/7		Continued wire cutting. Enemy retaliated on our front line trenches. A/189 & B/189 were put in this B.G.	Fine hot. Wym.
	18/7		ordered to distribute our entire & 20% shrapnel unless on great ingency.	Casualties 1 wounded B/III

Army Form C. 2118.

WAR DIARY
or
INTELLIGENCE SUMMARY.
(Erase heading not required.)

169 Bde RFA(Hy) page 5.

Instructions regarding War Diaries and Intelligence Summaries are contained in F.S. Regs., Part II. and the Staff Manual respectively. Title pages will be prepared in manuscript.

Place	Date	Hour	Summary of Events and Information	Remarks and references to Appendices
Nr ARMENTIERES.	19/7		Ordered to continue wire cutting up to 1000 Rds shrapnel/p/p/gun.	W/w.
	20/7		Ordered not to shoot unless of special order.	V. fine day. W/c/s.
	21/7		Enemy artillery fairly active. Shelled many localities but without much effect.	Very fine. Wind N-NE. Casualties + men wounded. W/w.
	22/7		Fairly quiet day.	Fine wind N.
	23/7	5.30 P.M.	Batteries again ordered to start wire cutting as formerly. Bty 89 13/189. Orders Sent with S.O. for about 2 hours. No casualties.	W/w.
	24/7		Wire cutting continued.	". Fine wind N.
	25/7		" " "	Fine cloudy wind NW.
	26/7	6 PM	Further wire cutting by A/1 8 3 + M. J. M. C/169 A/169 by orders & energetic fire Batt	" " " for cable.

Army Form C. 2118.

WAR DIARY
or
INTELLIGENCE SUMMARY. /89 Bde RFA   July page 6
(Erase heading not required.)

Place	Date	Hour	Summary of Events and Information	Remarks and references to Appendices
In action N of ARMENTIERES	July 26th/15	11 P.M.	Bombardment of enemy's trenches commenced.	
		11.30	Raid of party of 2nd D.L.I. left our trenches about C.4.d.0.5. & Coy down in front.	
		12 M.N.	Btys. raised their fire as an afform barrage behind enemy's support line. Infants were supposed to enter enemy front line trenches, left half [?] in all respect but in part of centre portion which had been heavily shelled by enemy while lying out in "No Mans Land" had suffered heavy casualties failed to get in, but T.C. said reports to OC enterprise that the Coyhn was helpless, ordered men to retire. Lt. BENEST A/189 attached to OC Enterprise as Liason Officer did very good work in keeping up communications with Bn. & Bde HQ after the line from front line to Bn. HQ had been cut. There was a retaliation by enemy artillery on the Batteries. D/189 had a premature or muzzle of gun which blew away piece of shield & caused 5 casualties. 1 man killed D/189 three wounded.	

Army Form C. 2118.

WAR DIARY
or
INTELLIGENCE SUMMARY.
(Erase heading not required.)

169 Inf. Bde. H.Q. July page 7.

Instructions regarding War Diaries and Intelligence Summaries are contained in F. S. Regs., Part II. and the Staff Manual respectively. Title pages will be prepared in manuscript.

Place	Date	Hour	Summary of Events and Information	Remarks and references to Appendices
In action No 2 ARMENTIERES	27/7		a very quiet day.	
	28/7		ditto	Weather fine hot wind N.W.5 N.
	29/7		ditto	ditto
	30/7		ditto	Fine hot.
	31/7		ditto	Fine hot.

Murellisane

31/7/16. Army 189 Bde Pg.

Army Form C. 2118.

41/ Vol 4

WAR DIARY
of 189 Bde RFA
INTELLIGENCE SUMMARY.

(Erase heading not required.)

Instructions regarding War Diaries and Intelligence Summaries are contained in F. S. Regs., Part II. and the Staff Manual respectively. Title pages will be prepared in manuscript.

Aug. page 1.

Place	Date	Hour	Summary of Events and Information	Remarks and references to Appendices
N of ARMENTIERES.	1916 AUG 1"		A quiet day.	V Hot. misty. hur.
	2"	2-6 P.M.	A/189. 3. C/189. D/189 shelled X55 killed about C6 B50. wit aeroplane observation.	V Hot. misty. hur.
	2"	9.43	Shelled with about boubs of five roads in vicinity of DOULEMENT - hyer.	
		10.37	PONT ROUGE - LES ECLUSES.	
		10.59		♯ V. hot.
		11.23		
	3"		A quiet day	cooler.
	4"		ditto.	
	5"		"	
	6"		Aeroplanes on both sides very active today.	warmer. hur
	7"		normal activity.	
	8"	10.32 PM	Road shoot as carried out on 2" been again carried out	to cooler.
		11.2		
		11.41		
		12.14 AM		

Army Form C. 2118.

WAR DIARY
or
INTELLIGENCE SUMMARY. 189 Bde CFA.
Aug, page 2
(Erase heading not required.)

Instructions regarding War Diaries and Intelligence Summaries are contained in F. S. Regs., Part II. and the Staff Manual respectively. Title pages will be prepared in manuscript.

Place	Date	Hour	Summary of Events and Information	Remarks and references to Appendices
N of ARMENTIERES	Aug. 1916 9c.	AM 8.30	At LE BISET - C/189 shelled S.S.9" until about 2.30 P.M. Between 3.00 & 6.00 shells dropped & have been fired. C/189 fired 600 rounds of one per pit. Horses in but no casualties as detachments had been removed or commencement of shelling. Retaliated on suspected BFs. their own shelling with D/189 & A/189. Also retaliated on front line trenches with B/189 & A/189. A very hot day.	hyper.
	10c		quiet day.	hyper.
	11c		" "	
	12c		" "	vher.
	13c		" "	Cornallis B/189 wounded (accidentally) hyper.
	14c		" "	
	15c		" "	
	16		" "	Storey
	17		" "	hyper.

Army Form C. 2118.

WAR DIARY
or
INTELLIGENCE SUMMARY.

/89 Bde RFA.
Aug. page 3.

(Erase heading not required.)

Place	Date	Hour	Summary of Events and Information	Remarks and references to Appendices
No. 8 ARMENTIERES.	Aug. 18.		O.C. 104" Bde RFA arrived & take over. Quiet day.	
	19"	8 PM	Head Qrs. of 104" Bde RFA relieved.	
	20"	8 PM	One section of each Bty relieved ditto	
	21"	8 AM	2nd section of each Bty ditto	
			HQ. 189 Bde RFA having handed over to 104 Bde RFA Cap'n @ B.12 Central, en route for EECKE.	
EECKE.	22, 23		Resting at EECKE.	
	24"	12 MN	started for GODEWAERSVELDE Stn (line entraining)	
		2.0 M	reached ABBEVILLE. Batteries marched to COCQUEREL	
			Batteries followed at intervals of 3 hours.	
COCQUEREL	25"		Rested after journey	
	26 & 9 am		Battery Drill orders and training	
	27"		Individual Battery training. 2 Battery Commanders and 1 Officer from each battery visited (Somme Battle)	Very wet weather
	28"		" " " " " " " " " " " "	
	29 & 9 am		Brigade marching orders and tactical scheme.	
	30"		" " " "	
	31st		O.C. Brigade, one officer of each Battery and two Battery Commanders visited Somme Battle.	

W.M. Kellie
Lt Col
Comdg 189 Bde RFA

Vol 5
4/st
189. H. Bde RFA
September 1916
Army Form C. 2118.
Page 1.

WAR DIARY or INTELLIGENCE SUMMARY.
(Erase heading not required.)

Place	Date	Hour	Summary of Events and Information	Remarks and references to Appendices
COCQUEREL	Sept. 1916 1st	7.30 pm	Brigade marched to Argoeures.	
ARGOEUVRES	2nd	2:00 am	Brigade arrived and went into Bivouac	
"	2nd	8.30 PM	Brigade marched to DERNANCOURT.	
DERNANCOURT	3rd	6 am	Brigade arrived at DERNANCOURT and Bivouaced. Rested.	2/Lt.B.L. ROSHER evacuated sick
"	4th			
"	5th		O.C. Brigade and Battery Commanders reconnoitred positions near BAZENTIN-LE-GRAND, for line of fire in direction of FLERS. Working parties were left to prepare positions.	
BAZENTIN LE GRAND	6th evening		Brigade occupied positions, wagon lines near ALBERT. Brigade Headquarters established in BAZENTIN-LE-GRAND Wood.	Fine weather
"	7th		Batteries	
"	8th		Ballines entrenched	
"	9th		" Registered. Centre of zone allotted to Bde passes through FLERS.	Casualties 2 Rank & file wounded.
"	10th		" Registration continued.	Casualties 2/Lt H.L.ROBERTS died of wounds. 2/Lt J.W. DAVIS wounded accidentally 2 Other ranks wounded

Army Form C. 2118.

WAR DIARY
or
INTELLIGENCE SUMMARY.
(Erase heading not required.)

189 Bde RFA.   Sept Page 2.

Place	Date	Hour	Summary of Events and Information	Remarks and references to Appendices
BAZENTIN LE GRAND	Sept. 11th		Bde ordered to fire SD 2 rounds 18 Pr, & 2 rounds Howitzer ammunition by day	Casualties
	12th		and 6 & 4 " " " night	1 other rank wounded.
			Batteries (18 Prs) ordered to cut wire in their zone. Howitzers to bombard hostile batteries, continuing day & night bombardment as above. CAPT. H.H. HARFORD evacuated sick.	1 other rank wounded.
	13th		Wire cutting and bombardment continued.	
	14th		" "	
	15th 6.20 AM		"zero hour". XV Corps, of which 41 Divn in part, attacked.	1 other rank wounded.
			(1). FLINT TRENCH from ALE ALLEY & TEA SUPPORT & COFFEE LANE about S 5 d 8 2 & CREST TRENCH as far west as S 5 c 4 5	
			(2). SWITCH TRENCH from T 6 a 2 0 4 5 to S 5 central.	
			(3). GAP TRENCH from T 2 1 2 6 - FLERS TRENCH as far west as M 36 c 4 3 & M 36 c 2 7 along trench running west from M 36 c 2 7 - FAT TRENCH TRENCH from M 36 c 4 3 to M 36 c 2 7 along trench running west from M 36 c 2 7- road junction at M 35 d 9 8.	
			(4). Road from Flers Trench junction at N 32 d 9 0 1 5 - N 31 b 4 0 - thence	

Army Form C. 2118.

Sent page 3

WAR DIARY
or
INTELLIGENCE SUMMARY. /89 Bde RFA.
(Erase heading not required.)

Place	Date	Hour	Summary of Events and Information	Remarks and references to Appendices
BAZENTIN LE GRAND	Sept 15th		FLERS village & communication trench (GROVE ALLEY) as far as N 30 d 3.5 (5). The GEUDECOURT line from N 32 a 90 15 to N 19 a 84. & GEUDECOURT village. A/189. Took part in creeping Barrage. (See appendix S.45). B & C/189 " " " " " " " The 41st Div succeeded in capturing FLERS but did not succeed in 5th objective. Div was complimented on work performed.	
	16th		Another attack was ordered on GEUDECOURT & GIRD TRENCH by another Div.	6 other ranks wounded
			For this they "41st" Div Arty being ordered to cooperate. Orders attached (S/30). It was not successful. A/189 & D/189 ordered to move into DELVILLE WOOD.	
	17th	5 pm	Bde ordered to take up position about S.8 & c.d. & be in action by 5 pm. 185.A/189 & more than also.	1 other rank killed, 3 other ranks wounded
No. 9. 1000 W# LONGUEVAL	18th		Rain came on & it was with great difficulty guns were got into position. Heavy rain all day ground became almost impassible & per up ammunition to guns was a very difficult task, men & horses much exhausted. MGs registered & fired on orders.	Capt. K.F.M.DUNN wounded see DA 16 attached
	19th		Heavy rain at intervals. The mud colossal. No material could be got up.	3 other ranks wounded

Army Form C. 2118.

WAR DIARY or INTELLIGENCE SUMMARY.

189 ссе RFA

Sept page 4.

(Erase heading not required.)

Place	Date	Hour	Summary of Events and Information	Remarks and references to Appendices
1000 x W of LONGUEVAL Sept.	Sept 20		Provide shelter for the men &c as every available horse was required to get up ammunition. Both officers & men suffered a great deal from exposure. From arrival in position M.G.s were shelled intermittently day & night. Only cover was an infantry trench beside which guns were placed, it was full of water & had no head cover. M.G. Registered & continued day & night shooting as detailed.	
	20.		Heavy showers at intervals. Cold. Normal shooting. 2/Lt H.E. McKIE evacuated sick casualties	
	21.		Slight rain, cold. Head Qrs. shelled 3.45 PM & 6 PM, 4.2 & tear shell. at intervals p.m.	4 other ranks wounded
	22.		Fine, sunny.	1 Other rank killed, 1 other rank wounded
	23.		Fine, warm, sunny. Things clearing up a bit. Hd Qrs & surrounding camps shelled.	1 other rank wounded
	24.	AM 7	Bombardment as ordered in 41st Div Art. O.O. No 17 of 21.9.16 started.	✱ 1 copy attached to original copy of diary.
		PM 6.30	Bombardment ceased & ordinary rapid firing took place. weather fine, heavy in hurry but leaving early	4 other ranks wounded

Army Form C. 2118.

WAR DIARY
or
INTELLIGENCE SUMMARY. 189 Bde RFA.
(Erase heading not required.)

~~See~~ Sept page 5

Instructions regarding War Diaries and Intelligence Summaries are contained in F.S. Regs., Part II. and the Staff Manual respectively. Title pages will be prepared in manuscript.

Place	Date	Hour	Summary of Events and Information	Remarks and references to Appendices
HR. 1000 x W 0. LONGUEVAL	Sept 25.	A.M. 6.30	Bombardment recommences & continues till zero hour.	
		P.M. 12.35	Zero Hour. 55th Div. regs of three Zone 189" Bde in evening attacks line N.26 b 5.7. to N.19.c.9.1. 21st Div. on right attacks N.34.a.2.2 to N.26 b 5.7. inclusive to GUEDECOURT VILLAGE. NEWZEALAND Div. on left attacks N 19.c.9.1. to M.24.c.6.0. Barrages established as laid down in Appendix 6.4 to DA.O.O. no 17. of 23.9.16.* All objectives eventually attained.	*1 copy attached to original war diary. Fine sunny.
	26"		Ordinary firing & wire cutting on GIRD TRENCH in Bde Zone.	Fine sunny.
	27"	7.A.M.	D/189. commenced bombardment of strong points in zone.	
		P.M. 2.15	A. B & C M.G. commenced creeping barrage as detailed in 41.D.A.O.O. no 18. Infy advance & capture GIRD TRENCH & GIRD SUPPORT in N19 B & D. F.O.O. reported that Infy appeared to find no difficulty in getting through wire. As Germans were reported massing in N.13 this area was searched & barrage maintained till after 8PM. D/189 had ammunition in 3 1⁄2 Pdr gun pits cut on fire & 3 guns damaged. 5 shell fire (only 1 man wounded).	

Army Form C. 2118.

WAR DIARY
or
INTELLIGENCE SUMMARY.

189th Bde R.F.A. Sept page 6.

(Erase heading not required.)

Place	Date	Hour	Summary of Events and Information	Remarks and references to Appendices
H.Q. 1000 x W. of LONGUEVAL.	Sept 28		normal firing	Casualties: 2Lr. A.W. BLACKDEN Killed 1 Other rank wounded
	29.		Ordinary day and night firing. a very wet day.	Major G.B. OWER Killed 1 Other rank wounded.
	30		Ordinary day and night firing	M W Reid Lt Col Comdg 189 Bde R.F.A. 30.9.16.

ARTILLERY
41st DIVISIONAL F/O. DR. NO. 14

SECRET.

1. Infantry will attack GIRD TRENCH and GIRD SUPORT tomorrow Sept 16th starting from their present position - line NORTH of FLERS VILLAGE - at 9.25 a.m.

2. A creeping barrage will be established on the line N.31.b.9.7 to N.25.c.9½.5½ and 9.15 am and remain on this line till 9.25 a.m.

3. A stationary barrage will be established at 9.15 a.m. on the line N.26.c.4.5 to N.25.a.8.3

4. The Left flank of the creeping barrage will advance at the rate of 40^X per minute the Centre and Right at the rate of 30^X per minute opening out until it covers the entire line of the stationary barrage at the points mentioned in para 3. The creeping barrage will continue to advance until it rests upon the line
   N.26.c.4.5. to N.19.d.3.9
reaching the left of the line at N.19.d.3.9 at 9.55 a.m.
The creeping barrage will lift off the GIRD TRENCH between N.26.c.4.5. and N.26.c.3.7. at 9.44 a.m. and search back 200^X by lifts of 100^X per minute remaining on this line till 10.30 a.m.
The creeping barrage from N.26.c.3.7. to N.19.d.3.9 will remain on GIRD TRENCH till 10 a.m.
At 10 a.m. it will search back to a line
   N.13.c.0.0 to N.21.c.3.8.
by lifts of 100^X every minute and remain there till further orders.
At 10.30 a.m. the guns on the line 200^X beyond the points N.26.c.4.5 and N.26.c.3.7 will lift direct to the barrage line N.13.c.0.0 to N.21.c.3.8 and remain there till further orders.

5. The creeping barrage will be established by advanced groups under
   Lt.Col. Head and Lt.Col Fitzgerald,
The dividing line between the groups will be :-
   N.25.d.3.2. - N.20.a.5.3. - N.20.a.7½.2½
Colonel Head taking right portion
Colonel Fitzgerald taking Left portion.
   20
Rates of fire 9.15 a.m. to 9.25 a.m. 3 rounds per gun per minute.
9.25 a.m. - 9.55 a.m.   2 rounds per gun per minute
9.55 a.m. - 10.0 a.m.   3 rounds per gun per minute
10 a.m. - 11 a.m.   1 round per gun per 2 minutes
11 a.m. till stopped   1 round per gun per 4 minutes

6. Stationary barrage:-
   (a) 9.15 a.m. to 9.25 a.m. on line N.26.c.4.5. to N.25.a.8.3.
   (b) Lifts at 9.25 a.m. to N.26.c.6.6. to N.19.c.9.1 until 9.35 a.m.
   (c) Lifts at 9.35 a.m. to N.26.c.6.6. to N.19.b.3.2. until 9.40 am
   (d) At 9.40 a.m. searches back 200^X and remains on that line till 10.30 a.m.
   (e) At 10.30 a.m. stationary barrage ceases.

7. The stationary barrage will be carried out by the two 18-pr Btys 183 Bde. which have not moved,
   (a) Right Group 21st D.A. 189 & 190 Bdes R.F.A. dividing lines as under :-
   183 Bde. EAST of a line N.26.c.2½.5½ to N.26.a.8½.3½ up to Divisional Boundary on the Right.

(b) Right Group 21st D.A. from above line to a line along GLASS LANE N.25.d.5.9 to N.20.c.6½.7½.

(c) 189 & 190 Bdes. from above line to Divisional Boundary on the Left.

Rates of fire

9.15 a.m. to 9.30 a.m. 3 rounds per gun per minute
9.20 a.m. to 9.35 a.m. 2   "   "   "   "
9.35 a.m. to 10.30 a.m. 1   "   "   "   " 2 minutes

8. (a) Howitzer btys will bombard GIRD TRENCH and GIRD SUPPORT from 6 a.m. until 9.40 a.m. at 1 round per gun per 3 minutes in the zones allotted to them for operations Sept. 15th
(b) Howr. Btys of 189, 190 Bdes and Left Group 21st D.A. will continue bombardment until 9.50 a. m. when they will switch to a line:-
N.19.central - M.24.b.5.5 continuation of GIRD TRENCH and GIRD SUPPORT each battery will take 250^x front 189 on the right, 190 centre, left Group 21st D.A. on left. Bombardment will continue at 1 round per gun per 2 minutes till 10.20 a.m.

(c) Howr Btys 183 and 187 Bdes and Right Group 21st D.A. will bombard GUEUDECOURT Village from 9.40 a.m. to 10.30 a.m. at 1 round per gun per 3 minutes

At 10.20 a.m. & 10.30 a.m. Howr Btys cease firing and come under orders of Bde and Group Commanders.

9. 190 Bde R.F.A. less C/190 with A/189 and D/189 under O.C. 190 Bde R.F.A will at once move to position SOUTH of FLERS Village about S.6.d. whence they can carry out wirecutting, barrages etc.
Every endeavour must be made to maintain touch with this Headquarters by orderlies to POZIERES. New position of Bde, and Batteries will be notified as early as possible.

10. Wire cutting will commence the moment the light permits.

11. ACKNOWLEDGE.

16-9-16.

Brigade Major
41st Divisional Artillery.

No. 1 41st Divsn.
 " 2 15th Corps R.A
 " 3 21st D.A.
 " 4 183 Bde. R.F.A
 " 5 187 "   "
 " 6 189 "   "
 " 7 190 "   "
 " 8 Left Group 21st D.A.
 " 9 Right "   "   "
 " 10 96th Bde. R.F.A. (c/o Left Group 21st D.A.)
 " 11 21st D.A.C.
 " 12 41st D.A.C
 " 13 O.C. Wagon Lines 41st D.A.
 " 14 O.C. "B" Dump
 " 15 T.M.C. 41st Divsn. thro' 183rd Bde. R.F.A
 " 16 7th D.A.
 " 17 14th D.A.

No. 18 122nd Inf. Bde.
 " 19 123   "   "
 " 20 124   "   "
    6 Spare.

(thro' 183rd Bde. R.F.A.)

1st DIVISIONAL ARTILLERY ORDER NO.10   1.

SECRET

                                                Ref. 1/20000 57c SW &
1.   XXXXXXXXXXXXXXXXXXXXX   Trench Maps

        At zero on "Z" day the XVth Corps, of which 41st Divsn
        forms a part, will attack.
        Time and date will be notified later

2.   The objectives of the XVth Corps are :-
        (i) PEAT TRENCH from ALE ALLEY to TEA SUPPORT, TEA
        SUPPORT to COFFEE LANE about S.5.d.8.2 and CREST TRENCH
        as far WEST as S.5.c.45.
        (ii) SWITCH TRENCH from T.8.a.20.45 to S.5.Central.
        (iii) GAP TRENCH from T.2.1.2.6 - FLEA TRENCH as far
        WEST as M.36.d.15.45 - FAT TRENCH - TRENCH from
        M.36.c.4.3. to M.36.c.2.7 - along Trench running WEST
        from M.36.c.2.7 to road junction at M.35.d.9.8.
        (iv) Road from Trench junction at N.32.d.90.15 to
        N.31.b.4.0 - the whole of FLERS Village and communication
        Trench (GROVE ALLEY) as far as M.30.d.3.5.
        (v) The GUEUDECOURT Line from N.32.d.90.15 to
        N.19.d.8.4 and GUEUDECOURT Village

3.   "Tanks" will be employed in 4 groups to assist the advance.
        It will be necessary to have gaps in the barrage to
        avoid hitting the tanks.

4.   The 18-pr barrage will be divided into two parts :-
        (a) Stationary
        (b) Creeping
        18-pr Btys. 41st & 21st D.As are allotted as under :-

        (a) Stationary Barrage :-
            187 Bde. R.F.A.   1 Battery
            Right Group 21st D.A. 4 batteries
            189 Bde. R.F.A.   2 batteries
            190 "   "   1 Bty.
            Left Group 21st D.A.   2 batteries.

        (b) Creeping Barrage :-
            183rd Bde R.F.A.   2 batteries
            187th "   "   1 Battery
            189th "   "   1 Battery
            190th "   "   1 Battery

        (c) At "disposal of C.R.A. :-
            183rd Bde R.F.A.   1 Battery
            187th "   "   1 "
            Left Group 21st D.A.   2 Batteries
        (d)
            Allotted to Counter Battery Group XVth Corps H.A.
            1 Battery (c) 190 Bde. R.F.A.
            4/ Hour Bty Left Group 21st DA

5.   "Stationary" barrage will be put up as follows :-
        (a) From zero hour to 6 minutes after zero hour
Stationary 187 Bde.   F.A.   ) (a) TEA SUPPORT TRENCH from
Barrage.   Right Group 21st D.A) T.47.a.16.62 to S.6.d.62.04.
0.0 to 0.6' 189 Bde. R.F.A.   )
            190 "   "   ) (b) TEA SUPPORT TRENCH from
            Left Group 21st D.A)   S.6.d.42.10, to S.6.c.60.23
                                     and (c) NEW TRENCH from
                                     S.6.c.05.00 to S.5.d.95.20

Rate of fire 3 rounds per gun per minute.

5 (cont) (b) At 6 minutes after zero hour stationary barrage will lift and search back quickly an increase of 50ˣ resting in SWITCH TRENCH as follows :-

0.6 - 0.30
EAST of
LONGUEVAL -
FLERS road
0.6 - 0.20
WEST of
LONGUEVAL
- FLERS road.

From 6 minutes after after zero hour to 30 minutes after zero hour EAST of LONGUEVAL - FLERS road and from 6 minutes after zero hour to 20 minutes after zero hour WEST of LONGUEVAL - FLERS Road as under

187 Bde. RFA   )(x) from T.1.d.00.25 to
Right Group 21st D.A   )   S.6.d.85.65

189 Bde. FA   )(y) From S.6.d.63.64 to   S.6.d.30-
190 "   "   )   S.6.c.90.54   50.
Left Group 21st D.A   (z) from S.6.c.68.60 to
                                S.6.c.3.7.

Rate of fire :- (1) from 0.10' to 0.12, 3 rounds per gun per minute.
                (2) from 0.12' to 0.20' or 0.30' 1½ rounds per gun per minute.

Batteries will open out their fire as necessary to cover the whole ground allotted.

6.
0.20 (or 0.30)
to
1.25 (or 1.30)
Stationary
Barrage.

At 30 minutes after zero hour stationary barrage EAST of LONGUEVAL - FLERS Road, and at 20 minutes after zero hour stationary barrage WEST of LONGUEVAL -FLERS Road Lift off SWITCH TRENCH and search back quickly to a line :-
(x) from T.1.b.15.25   to T.1.a.40.30
(y) from S.6.b.95.65   to S.6.b.65.85
(z) from S.6.b.45.95   to M.36.d.2.4

On arrival at these lines Btys sweep and cover lines as under :-

187 Bde. R.F.A.   ) From T.1.b.15.25 to T.1.a.1.6
Right Group 21st D.A.   )

189 Bde. R.F.A.   )
190 "   "   ) From T.1.a.1.6 to M.36.d.2.4
Left Group 21st D.A   )

remaining on these lines till, 1 hour 25 mins after zero, except the position N.WEST of point M.36.d.4.0 which remains on this line till 1 hour 30 minutes after zero.
Rates of fire :-
0.20' or 0.30' to 1.0 hour 1½ rounds per gun per minute.
1.0 hour to 1.25 hours or 1.30 hours 1 round per gun per minute.

7.
Stationary
Barrage
1.25 hours
and 1.30 hours
to
5.0 hours

At 1 hour 25. minutes after zero 187 Bde Right Group 21st D.A. 189 Bde. R.F.A. and batteries of Left Group 21st D.A. firing east of M.36.d.4.0. and at 1 hour 30 minutes after zero remaining Btys Left Group 21st D.A.
Search back quickly by lifts of 50ˣ until they reach a line :-
N.31.b.65.30 - N.31.a.25.95
On arrival at this line all batteries lift direct to the GUEUDECOURT LINE from
N.26.c.4.5. to N.19.d.3.9.

N.31.b.0.5
- N.31.a.5.7

7 (Cont.)	187 Bde. F.A.) covering from	
	Right Group 21st D.A.) N.26.c.4.5 - N.26.c.3.9.	
	189 Bde. F.A) covering from	N.90 E./5.45.
	190 Bde. ")	
	Left Group 21st D.A.) N.26.a.3.9. - N.19.d.3.9.	

These batteries also search and sweep to cover sup prt trench about 150x in rear of and parallel to this line.

<u>Rate of fire</u> (1) from 1 hour 25 min after zero to 1 hour 45 mins after zero... 1 round per gun per minute.
(2) From 1 hour 45 mins after zero to 4 hours after zero ..... 1 round per gun per 4 minutes.
(3) From 4 hours after zero to 5 hours after zero
    1 round per gun per 1½ minutes

8.
Stationary Barrage
5.0 hours to 5.30 hours

At 5 hours after zero all stationary barrage guns search back by 50^x increases to a distance of 200^x then (a)

1 battery 187 Bde. F.A) turn onto GUEUDECOURT
2 Btys Right Group 21st D.A.) village and the two
1 Bty 189 Bde. F.A.) roads leading into it
                            from the SOUTH WEST until
                            5 hours 30 mins after zero.

(b) remaining Btys of stationary barrage sweep to cover whole Divisional zone on this line exclusive of GUEUDECOURT Village

<u>Rate of Fire</u> From 5 hours after zero to 5 hours 30 mins after zero :-
    1 round per gun per 1½ minutes

9. At 5 hours 30 minutes after zero fire ceases.

10.
Creeping Barrage.
0.0 to 0.6'

Creeping barrage will be put up as follows:-
From 0.0 to 6 minutes after zero hour
(a) 183 Bde. F.A.) about 120^x (if safe) in front of
    187 Bde. R.F.A.) TEA SUPPORT trench from about
                    S.12.b.90.50 to S.12.b.60.65
(b) 189 Bde. F.A (about 120^x (if safe) in front of
                    TEA SUPORT trench from about
                    S.12.b.1.9½ - S 6.c.7.1.
(c) 190 Bde. F.A.... From about S.6.c.05.00 to
                    S.5.d.95.15.

creeping barrage 0.6 to 1.0

At 6 minutes after zero hour creeping barrage searches back by lifts of 50 yds every minute opening out and sweeping as necessary to a line :-

(a) T.1.d.25.80 - T.1.a.15.15
(b) S.6.b.70.20 - S.6.b.35.15
(c) S.6.b.20.10 - S.6.a.70.20

On arrival on these lines fire will be opened out to cover entire "Brigade" zone.
Until arrival at this line, gaps will be most carefully kept, as they are required for tanks to work in.

<u>Rate of fire</u>
    from zero hour to 0.12' 3 rounds per gun per minute.
    from 0.12.to.1.0 hour 2 rounds per gun per minute

4.

11. Creeping barrage 1.0 to 1.45

At one hour after zero creeping barrage batteries lift back by increases of 50^X every 1½ minutes being careful to cover the whole of their own brigade zones until they arrive at a line :-

183 Bde	F.A.	T.1.b.30.75	-	T.1.a.30.80
187	" "	T.1.a.80.80	-	N.31.c.40.10
189	" "	N.31.c.40.10	-	M.36.d.90.40
190	" "	M.36.d.90.40	-	M.36.d.60.90

Time 1.0 hour to 1.45'
Rate of fire 1 round per gun per minute.

12. Creeping barrage 1.45 to 4.15'

At 1 hour 45 minutes after zero the creeping barrage Batteries will search back by 100^X increases per minute until they arrive at a line as follows:-

183 BDE	F.A.	N.31.b.85.50	-	N.31.b.30.75
187	" "	N.31.b.30.75	-	N.31.b.00.85
189	" "	N.31.b.00.85	-	N.25.c.65.00
190	" "	N.25.c.65.00	-	N.25.c.35.15

Time from 1.45 to 4.15'
Rate of fire :-
   from 1.45' to 2.30' 1 round per gun per minute
    "   2.30' to 4.15' 1   "   "   "   " 3 minutes.

13. Creeping barrage 4.15' to 4.21'

At 4 hours 15 minutes after zero the batteries of the creeping barrage will search back by increases of 50 yards to a line 300 yards further back as under :-

183 Bde.	F.A.	N.25.c.25.05.	-	N.25.d.75.40
187	" "	N.25.d.75.40	-	N.25.d.35.65
189	" "	N.25.d.35.65	-	N.25.d.1.8
190	" "	N.25.d.1.8	-	N.25.a.7.0

Rate of fire 1 round per gun per minute

At 4 hours 21 mins creeping barrage batteries cease firing and come under the order of C.R.A., 41st Divsn for such use as may be required.

14. 4.5 Hows.

4.5 HOWITZER BATTERIES.

Bombardment by 4.5" Howitzers will commence at 30 minutes before zero.

Tasks.

183rd Bde:- Sunken road T.1.d.21. to T.1.d.15.95 one battery 21st D.A. Right Group :- both forks of road from S.6.b.8.1 to T.1.a.25 and to S.6.b.95.65
187 Bde :- T.1.c.95. to T.1.a.43.
189 Bde :- GATE LANE from T.1.c.05.50 to T.1.b.12.
One 4.5 Howr battery 21st D.A. Left Group :-
      FLASH TRENCH S.6.d.75.95 to S.6.b.45.15
190th Bde :- SUNKEN Road and trenches
      S.6.d.25.75 to S.6.b.35.10.

Times.

183rd Bde. :- commence -0.30 : continue at 1 round per gun per minute till 0.8. then lift to SUNKEN ROAD from T.1.b.12 to T.1.a.80.30 until 1.0 hours at 1 round per gun per 2 mins.

187th Bde. R.F.A. :- Commence -0.30 at 1 round per gun per minute until 0.8' then lift to T.1.c.6.6 to T.1.a.4.5. until 1.0hrs at 1 round per gun per 2 mins.

189th Bde. R.F.A. :- Commence at -0.30 continue at 1 round per gun per min till 0.8 then lift to T.1.c.6.8. to T.1.b.12 until 1 hour at 1 round per gun per 2 minutes.

One bty Right Group 21st D.A. Commence at -0.30 at 1 round per gun per minute. At 0.8 shlow to 1 round per gun per 2 mins and continue to 1 hour.

One battery Left Group 21st D.A. commences -0.30 at 1 round per gun per min till 0.8 then lift to T.1.a.25.55 to T.1.a.00.75 and continue at 1 round per gun per 2 mins until one hour.

190 Bde :- Commence at -0.30 at 1 round per gun per minute till 0.8 lift to T.1.a.00.75 to S.6.b.77 continues at 1 round per gun per two minutes until 1 hour

4.5" Hr.   SECOND PHASE

At 1 hour after zero all Howitzer batteries will lift to the following line as under :-

183rd Bde   FLES VILLAGE N.31.c.75 to N.31.c.35.65

21st D.A. Right Group FLES Village N.31.c.35.65 to N.31.c.00.65
searching 150 yds in short lifts.

187 Bde. will assist 4.5 Howr. Battery 21st D.A until ordered to advance
Time 1 hour to 1.50.
Rate of fire 1 round per gun per 3 minutes

189 Bde FORT TRENCH N.31.C.00.65 to M.36.d.8.8.
190 "   FORT TRENCH from M 36.d.8.8. to
                                          M.36.b.70.05
21st D.A Left Group will assist 190th Bde if not ordered to advance.
Time 1 hour to 1 hour 50 minutes.
Rate of fire 1 round per 3 minutes

At 1.50 after zero.

183rd Bde. will lift to N.31.a.85.15. to N.31.a.5.2
21st D.A. Right Group will lift to N.31.a.5.2. to
                                    N.31.a.30.15
Searching 100 yards by short lifts
Time 1.50 to 2 hours 30 minutes after zero
rate of fire 1 round per 3 minutes.

189th Bde will lift to N.31.a.30.15. to N.31.a.1.2.
190th Bde will lift to N.31.a.1.2. to N.36.b.95.35.
Searching 150 yards by short lifts.
Time 1 hr 50 mins. to 2 hrs 30 mins.
Rate of fire 1 round per gun per 3 minutes.

At 2hrs 30 mins. all 4.5 Howr Batteries will lift to line as under:-

183rd Bde:- FLEA Trench from N.31.b.80.55. to N.31.b.20.65.
21st D.A.Right Group:- COX FOIT between N.31.b.0.8. and N.31.a.75.90.
189th Bde:- BOX FOIT between N.25.c.8.0. and N.25.c.6.3.
190 Bde The FLAME between N.25.c.75.15 and N.25.c.8.5 and N.25.C.6.3
Time 2 hrs 30 mins to 4 hrs.
Rate of fire 1 round per gun per 3 minutes.

At 4.hrs. all Howr Batteries will lift to GIRD Support from N.26.c.6.8. to N.19.b.3.2. taking the portions of Trench in Brigade zone.

Time 4 hrs to 5 hrs.
Rate of fire 1 round per gun per 3 minutes.
At 5 hrs. cease fire - Await orders.

15. "Disposal" At zero the 18 pr Batteries at disposal will open fire on of 18prs. lines as under.

183rd Bde:- On road from T.1.b.1.2. to N.31.b.4.0.
187th Bde:- On road from T.1.a.3.6. to N.31.b.15.15.
2 Batteries Left Group 21st D.A.:-
On FLERS Main Street from T.1.a.0.8. to N.31.a.35.15.
and from S.6.b.85.85. to N.31.a.2.2.

Time 0.0. to 1 hr.
Rate of fire 1 round per gun per minute.

At 1 hr to 3 hrs. or until ordered to advance, the Right Group will open fire on the continuation N.E. of the roads on which they were firing from N.31.b.4.0. and N.31.a.85.15. to a depth of 600 yards.

Left Group if ordered to advance during period 0.0. to 1 hr will do so, discontinuing the fire ordered in para.1. If not ordered to advance at the conclusion of 1 hr. they will fire on the same roads to a depth of 600 yards N.E. of N.31.a.35.15. and N.31.a.2.2. until 3 hours. Their fire will be discontinued if ordered to advance is received before 3 hours. If no advance has taken place by 3 hours, 18 prs will cease firing and await orders.

16. Great care is necessary in working out the Barrages and making sure that all officers understand them, so that damage to the tanks may be avoided.

17 /

19. "Z" day will be September 15th.
Zero time will be notified.

20. O.C. 183rd Bde. R.F.A. will allot tasks to Batteries of 183rd, and 187th Bdes, and Right Group 21st D.A.
O.C. 190th Bde R.F.A. will allot tasks to Batteries of 189th and 190th Bdes and Left Group 21st D.A.

21. F.O.O's of all Batteries not at "disposal" will take advantage of the forward move of the Infantry to advance with a view to obtaining better observation.

22. Acknowledge.

Major R.A.

14th Sept. 1916. Brigade-Major, 41st Divnl. Artillery.

Copies to:-

1 XV Corps R.A.
2 41st Div "G".
3   :   :   "Q".
4 21st D.A. (6 Copies).
5 183 Bde RFA
6 187 :
7 189 :
8 190 :
9 41st D.A.C.
10 O.C. "B" Dump.
11 T.M.C.
12. XV Corps H.A.
13 122nd Inf. Bde.
14 123rd :   :
15 124th :   :
16 Capt. Elsdale.
    3 spare.

SEC.FT.   VERY URGENT

                    Amendment to 41st Divl. Artillery
                           Order No. 10 of 14-9-16.

Amendment to   After.
para 10 (part 2)   "At 6 minutes after zero hour creeping barrage
Creeping   searches back by lifts of 50" every minute"
barrage   Insert.
0.6 to 1.0   "leaving the following gaps when crossing the
                       SWITCH TRENCH T.1.d.3.1 (outside area) to
                       T.1.c.8.3.
                       T.1.c.0.6.   to S.6.d.5.6.
                       S.6.d.2.5.   to S.6.c.6.6.

Amendment to   Amend para 14 as under :-
para 14
(4.5 hows)   (1) Bombardment by 4.5 Hows. will commence at 0.20
                        before zero.

                    (2) 183rd Bde. R.F.A.
                                     Cancel target
                        SUNKEN ROAD T.1.d.2.1 - T.1.d.15.95
                        ~~T.1.d.15.95~~
                        Substitute target S.12.b.95.70 - S.12.b.70.90
                                     TEA SUPPORT.

                    Cancel "Times 183rd Bde. "

                    Substitute.
                           183rd Bde. commence -20 continue at 1
                    round per gun per minute till 0 0. Then lift to
                    SUNKEN ROAD from T.1.b.1.2 to T.1.a.80.30 until
                    1.0 hours at 1 round per gun per 2 minutes.
                    The greatest care is to be taken to avoid damage
                    to tanks.

                    190 Brigade.
                                Cancel target SUNKEN ROAD & TRENCHES
                    S.6.d.25.75 - S.6.b.35.10.
                                Substitute target S.6.d.15.20 - S.6.c.75.20
                    TEA SUPPORT.

                    Cancel "TIMES 190 Brigade"
                    and substitute
                           Commence at -0.20 at 1 round per gun per min
                    till 0.8, then lift to T.1.a.25.55 - T.1.a.00.75 and
                    continue at 1 round per gun per 2 minutes until
                    1 hour.
                    The greatest care is to be taken to avoid damage to
                    tanks.

Circulated
Battys   *signature*   *signature*
3.30 a   Brigade Major
                    14-9-16.   41st Divisional Artillery.

                    Copy No. 1 XV Corps A.A.   No. 9 122nd Inf. Bde.
                         "   2 21st Divsn Q   " 10 123   "   "
                         "   3   "   "   G   " 11 124   "   "
                         "   4 21st D.A.   " 12 Right Group 21st DA
                         "   5 183 Bde.   " 13 Left   "   "   "
                         "   6 187 "   " 14 41st D.A.C.
                         "   7 189 "   " 15 T.M.C
                         "   8 190 "   " 16 XV Corps H.A.

DA 16.

41st DIVISION ARTILLERY O DR No. 16

SECRET

1. Until further orders commencing from 6.30 a.m. Sept 18th day and night firing will be carried out between the hours of:-
   day firing .... 6.30 a.m. to 6.30 p.m.
   night firing ... 6.30 p.m. to 6.30 a.m.

2. Ammunition allotment for day and night firing and wire cutting is shewn in para 3 & 4.

3. Ammunition allotted for day firing.
   (a) approximate allowance and distribution of 18-pr.

   Left Group 21st D.A. For wire cutting 600 for general use 200
   Right   "   "   "   "   "   "   Nil "   "   600
   183 Bde. 41st "   "   "   "   "   600 "   "   100
   187   "   "   "   "   "   "   "   Nil "   "   250
   189   "   "   "   "   "   "   "   Nil "   "   250
   190   "   "   "   "   "   "   "   Nil "   "   250

   Left Group 21st D.A., and 183rd Bde. will each endeavour to push up a forward gun or guns for wire cutting. Left Group 21st D.A. Left zone 183rd Bde. on right & Centre zones.
   Left Group 21st D.A. and 183rd Bde O/Cs will have these rounds fired from, forward, or present positions, in such proportions as they may consider most suitable.
   Every effort is to be made to avoid wasting ammunition in long distance wirecutting.
   Remainder of ammunition should be used for careful registration strong points, counter battery and fleeting opportunities.
   Wire cutting should be completed by 6 p.m. Sept 20th

   (b) Allowance of 4.5" How Ammn for day firing :-

   70 rounds per battery.

   To be used on careful registration, strong points, fleeting opportunities and counter battery work.

4. Ammunition for night firing :-

   Right Group 21st D.A.,   900
   Left   "   21st D.A.,   600
   183 Bde   41st D.A.,   Nil
   187 "   "   "   500
   189 "   "   "   500
   190 "   "   "   500

   4.5 Howitzers.   70 rounds per battery.

   Night firing will be carried out on similar lines as before.

5. At present care is required in not unduly expending ammunition but not less than 75% of the day allotment must be fired, while the whole of the night allowance must be fired.
   In event of a hostile attack NO limit is placed on expenditure

6. Above cancels all order for firing and allotments of ammunition previously issued - except that the creeping x barrage ordered in my S.39 of to-day for 11.30 a.m. Sept 18th will be carried out.
Ammunition used for this barrage will be extra to day allotment.

7. All batteries will endeavour to establish a 300 round dump per gun by 12 midnight 20th Sept.

8. The G.O.C., R.A., is fully aware of the great calls that have recently been made on the courage, skill and endurance of all ranks, which have been so splendidly responded to, and he is sure that all ranks will add to their fine reputation in any future operations

9. ACKNOWLEDGE.

[signature]

Brigade Major
41st Divisional Artillery.

17th Sept.
1 9 1 6.

```
No.  1   21st D.A.
 "   2   41st Divsn.
 "   3   55th    "
 "   4   XV Corps R.A.
 "   5   183 Bde. R.F.A.
 "   6   187  "    "
 "   7   189  "    "
 "   9   190  "    "
 "  10   Left Group  21st D.A.
 "  11   Right  "      "    "
 "  12   D.A.Cs 41st
 "  13   D.A.C  21st
 "  14   T. .C
 "  15   O/C Dump.
 "  16   164 Inf. Bde
 "  17   165  "    "
 "  18   166  "    "
 "  19   FILE
```

Army Form C. 2118.

VOL 6
Oct page 1.

WAR DIARY
or
INTELLIGENCE SUMMARY. 189 Bde RFA.
(Erase heading not required.)

Instructions regarding War Diaries and Intelligence Summaries are contained in F.S. Regs., Part II. and the Staff Manual respectively. Title pages will be prepared in manuscript.

Place	Date	Hour	Summary of Events and Information	Remarks and references to Appendices
HQ. 1000× W.B LONGUEVAL	Oct 1st		41" Div Arty now cover 21st Div frontage. Operation Today, Operation in A} N.Z. Div in attacking enemys trenches from M.24 b.0.5 - M.23 b.7.4 and establishing a line through N.19. G.5.3 - M.24. B.O.5 - M.24 B.7.5 - M.23 B.7.0 Connecting with III Corps on Right. 21st Div were not ordered to take an active Part as	Casualties. 2 other ranks Wounded.
		3pm	2000 hours intense enemy arty barrage put up by 41st Div arty on enemys depots. They now intend to pin forces to the front with a view to future operations	
		3.15	Zero hour. 41st Div Arty commenced Barrage as ordered in 1st Div. OO No 20 (copy attached)	
		5.30	Enemy reduced L.180 pr pr per gun 10min - 7.15 pm at Rifled mountain light firing (fine) 8 rounds (wet uncertainties)	
	2d		Normal firing. Reconnaissance of positions in advance carried out	
	3d		Normal firing. Reconnaissance continued	(very wet)
	4th		Orders for transmission to 4th rattacks on 5th prepared for 4.6 hour normal firing. Blfs started on new positions about M.3.5.b M.36.a. (Some rain)	
	5th		Normal firing	Casualties 1 other man Wounded

Army Form C. 2118.

WAR DIARY
or
INTELLIGENCE SUMMARY. 189 Bde R.F.A.   Oct page 2.
(Erase heading not required.)

Place	Date	Hour	Summary of Events and Information	Remarks and references to Appendices
HQ 10700	Oct 6th	3.15 PM	Bombardment commenced as ordered in BM 41. D.A.00. No 22. of 3.10.16 & amendment	of 5.10.16
W do		5.15 PM	During ad. received ord. hit. (Fine showery.)	
LONGUEVAL	7th	7.45 AM	When bombardment recommenced and continued till zero hour.	
		1.45 PM	(zero hour) 12th Division attacked as ordered in 12 Div OO. No 113 of 7.10.16.	
			Barrage barrage as ordered in 41. D.A.O.O. No 23. of 5.10.16. Thro' barrage carried	
			out be continued at a reduced rate of fire till about 2 P.M. when ic recommenced & stopped	
			at intervals up till 6 P.M. to keep down traffic & working parties about captured trenches.	
			Opened action as ordered in SOS line received in an zone from N 13 d.5.5. ("Bayonet" Trench	
			N. 20 a 2.8 on hostile opposition down not appear to have been severe) (Fine, showery.)	
	8th		Normal shooting. Rain more or less all day.	
	9th		" Fine, dull, chilly.	
	10th		Increased shooting ordered by Commander to can be put up to hew up for billets & all routes in villages yet any retire troops out. Very few have been found up to there for orders requested.	

WAR DIARY
or
INTELLIGENCE SUMMARY. 189th Bde RFA.

Army Form C. 2118.

see page 3.

Place	Date	Hour	Summary of Events and Information	Remarks and references to Appendices
HQ. 100ᵈ	Oct			
W.4	11ᵗʰ	AM		
LONGUEVAL		7	Bombardment commenced in accordance with 41.DA.O.O. no 24 of 10/10	
			& continued till zero hour on 12ᵗʰ	
	12ᵗʰ	PM 2.5	zero hour. Batteries barraged in accordance with 41.DA.OO. no 25 of 11/10	
		PM 8.30	Barrage which has been continued at a reduced rate for last 2 or 3 hours	Casualties
			has ceased to stop. Ordinary night firing to be continued.	1. O.R. killed.
			Fine, dull, coldish wind S.	
	13ᵗʰ		normal firing	cold clear, light rain.
	14ᵗʰ	PM 2.15	Short bombard as detailed in 41.DA.OO. no 26 of 13.10.16.	starts again.
		3.5	completed	
		11.PM about 6.	5.9 shell fell in vicinity of A B & C btys. throwing up a dump of 540 rounds in C Bty. no casualties	
			+41. DA.OO no 29. of 15.10.16.	
	15ᵗʰ		13 shrps fired in aerodrome with 41.DA.60. 20 27 of 14.10.16. & 41.DA.OO 20 28 of 14.10.	Casualties
			wet cold.	1. O.R. wounded
	16ᵗʰ		normal firing	fine evening, cold.

Army Form C. 2118.

WAR DIARY
or
INTELLIGENCE SUMMARY. 169 Bde R.F.A. Oct page 4.
(Erase heading not required.)

Instructions regarding War Diaries and Intelligence Summaries are contained in F. S. Regs., Part II. and the Staff Manual respectively. Title pages will be prepared in manuscript.

Place	Date	Hour	Summary of Events and Information	Remarks and references to Appendices
H.Q. 1000× W.q.	Oct 17		Ordinary firing. Bombardment as ordered in 41 D.A.O.O. no 30 of 16.10.16. Fine morning. Rain in evening.	Casualties 2 O.R. wounded.
LONGUEVAL	18		Battery fired as directed in 41 D.A.O.O. no 31 of 17.10.16. Monster Rain.	
	19"		Normal shooting. Rain all day.	
	20		Normal shooting. Between 1pm & 4pm. 3 5.9" shells fell in Bn H.Q. area close to Officers dugout. Frost in morning. N. wind & cold. Sunny.	2 O.R. wounded.
	21		Normal shooting. Frost in morning. N wind & cold. Sunny.	3 O.R. wounded
	22		" " N - N.E wind sunny.	
	23		Series bombardment of BAYONET TRENCH ordered. Cancelled with the difficulty of ammun supply & physical exhaustion of men. Rain in evening.	
	24		ditto. Operation for 25" postponed to 26". Rain 6th day.	
	25		Operation for 26" postponed to 28". Rain.	

Army Form C. 2118.

WAR DIARY
or
INTELLIGENCE SUMMARY. /89 Bde RFA
(Erase heading not required.)

Out page 5

Place	Date	Hour	Summary of Events and Information	Remarks and references to Appendices
HQ 100 x W of LONGUEVAL	Oct 26		Operations for 26th postponed to 30th. Firing to continue as ordered on 23rd.	
	27		Firing as usual. Rain as usual.	
	28		" " " Fine, dull, high wind S.	
	29		Operation for 30th postponed to 1st Nov. Firing as usual	
	30		" " " very wet.	
	31		One section per battery relieved by 22 Australian Field Artillery and proceeded to Waggon Lines. Fine, some rain	

W.H.Somerville
Major
Cdg 189 Brigade
Royal Field Artillery

Army Form C. 2118.

WAR DIARY
or
INTELLIGENCE SUMMARY.
(Erase heading not required.)

189 Bde R. November
PAGE 1.

Vol 7

Place	Date	Hour	Summary of Events and Information	Remarks and references to Appendices
	1916 Nov.			
MONTAUBAN.	1st	6am	Headquarters and remaining sections of Batteries marched to billets	Cremation 7th Thursday
			Headquarters and Band C Battery at LA NEUVILLE. A and D Batteries at BONNAY.	provided (dipped of wounds afternoon) weather fine
LA NEUVILLE	2nd		Brigade in billets as above.	showery.
	3rd.	7.15	Brigade marched to TALMAS and went into billets.	fine
TALMAS	4th.	9.40am	Brigade marched to AMPLIER and billetted.	fine
AMPLIER	5th.	8.20am	Brigade marched to BOUBERS-SUR-CANCHE and billetted.	fine.
BOUBERS.	6th.	7.40am	Brigade marched to HEUCHIN and billetted.	wet wet. I.O.R. accidently injured.
HEUCHIN	7th.		Brigade in billets at HEUCHIN. 2LT. HOLDER & 2LT. G. LAMB evacuated sick.	
	8th.	"	"	
	9th.	7.35am	Brigade marched to BERGUETTE and billetted.	fine I.O.R. injured accidently
BERGUETTE	10h.	9.45am 8am	Brigade marched to WALLON CAPPEL and billetted. Advance party of Brigade Commander, Adjutant, Battery Commanders and one Subaltern per battery, and telephonists went forward to new positions near ST. EL OI.	

T.2134. Wt. W708—776. 500000. 4/15. Sir J. C. & S.

Army Form C. 2118.

NOV. PAGE 2.

WAR DIARY
or
INTELLIGENCE SUMMARY.
(Erase heading not required.)

Place	Date	Hour	Summary of Events and Information	Remarks and references to Appendices
WALLON-CAPPEL	11th	9am	Brigade marched to GODWAERSVELDE and billeted.	weather fine
GODWAERSVELDE	12th		Right sections of batteries marched to positions near DICKEBUSCHE and relieved right sections of 10th Australian Field Artillery Brigade fine weather. Remainder of Brigade in billets.	
			MAJOR. G.M. SPENCER-SMITH wounded.	
H.Q. 500 yards N.E. of DICKEBUSCHE	13th		Remaining sections of batteries relieved remaining sections of 10th A.F.A. Bde. Took over command of Lt. E.L.O1 GROUP artillery, consisting of A/189, B/189, C/189, D/189, A/183, B/183, C/183, D/183, 3 "75" Belgian batteries 17th Regt. F.A. 1 and 2 Medium Trench Mortar Batteries.	
			Right sections commenced registration.	weather fine but misty. Visibility poor.
			Registration continued	" fine. Visibility good between 12.30 - 3 P.M.
"	14th		"	" " Visibility good throughout.
"	15th		"	"
"	16th		Took over command of 183 Brigade R.F.A. for administrative purposes as well as fighting purposes, in addition to 189 Bde. R.F.A.	
"			Registration continued	weather fine
"	17th		Registration continued. Ammunition allotment 6 rounds per gun per day only.	
		3pm	Wire cutting commenced by Medium Trench Mortars. Covering fire provided by 18pdrs + 4.5 Hows.	

Army Form C. 2118.
NOV. PAGE 3.

WAR DIARY
or
INTELLIGENCE SUMMARY.
(Erase heading not required.)

Place	Date	Hour	Summary of Events and Information	Remarks and references to Appendices
H.Q. 500 yds N.E. of PICKE-BUSCHE	18th	8am	Wire cutting continued by Medium Trench Mortars. Covering fire provided by 151dis 9 & 5 Hours.	wet. 1 O.R. found drowned.
	19th	3.30pm	" " " "	wet
	20th	8am	ditto	
	21st	2.15pm	ditto	
		2.15am	Batteries fired "dummy raid" bombardments as ordered in 41 D.A. Operation Order No. 40.	foggy
	22nd	3.15	Wire cutting continued by M.T.Ms	"
			Covering fire provided	"
	23	2.5.	Wire cutting by M.T.M and covering fire	misty
	24		" " "	"
	25		" " "	"
	26		" " "	reorganisation commenced showers
	27		Ordinary fire	reorganisation completed close of D/183 fire
	28		" "	(retired to Wagon lines) foggy

Army Form C. 2118.

NOV Page 4

WAR DIARY
or
INTELLIGENCE SUMMARY
(Erase heading not required.)

Place	Date	Hour	Summary of Events and Information	Remarks and references to Appendices
H.Q. 500 yards.				
N.E.of	29.	11.30am	Fired in accordance with H.Sec Arty O.O. No 42.	foggy
DICKEBUSCHE		1.30pm	Wire cutting by M.T.Mo. + evening fire	
30K./2.30pm			" " "	fine but misty

Murray
Lt Col R.F.A.
ag 189 Bde RFA.

To:- Officers Commanding,
    A, C & D/187

    Reference attached.
    A/187 will comply with Schedule A paras A. B. F. & G.
    C/187   ditto   C. D. H. & I.
    D/187   ditto   C and J.

                                            [signature]
                                            Lieut. & Adj.
26/11/16.   St. Eloi Arty. Group.

To:- Officers Commanding,
    A, B, C and D/187

    Beginning tomorrow morning 27th inst., batteries will have working parties at work on their new positions as follows:-
        A/187 at SANDBAG & RAVINE
        B/187 at its own position (SCOTCH)
        C/187 at BOLLARD
        D/187 at H 36.c.7.4

    Work on the new positions must be pushed on as quickly as possible.

                                            [signature]
                                            Lieut. & Adjt, R.F.A.
26/11/16   St. Eloi Arty. Group, R.F.A.

To:- Officer Commanding,
    B/187th, Bde. R.F.A.

    Attached in relation to work to be done at a new trench O.P. in the blind trench (by the M.G. emplacement) just off the Old Kent Road about O.3.b.1½.5½. Preliminary work, namely excavating and revetting of the space excavated must be proceeded with at once. Work must be begun to-morrow morning (27th. inst.) and completion reported to this office.

                                            [signature]
26/11/16   St. Eloi Arty. Group, R.F.A.

SECRET

Ref. Map WYTSCHAETE
28 S.W. 2 1/10,000

41st DIVISIONAL ARTILLERY OPERATION
ORDER No. 42.

INTENTION.
1. The 41st Divisional Artillery will destroy hostile trench Mortars at C.8.a.7.4 and N.18.b.9½.3½ on November 29th 1916.

TACTICS.
2. A square barrage will be placed all round these mortars which will take in trenches near them, thus blocking all exits, meanwhile the mortars will be bombarded by 4.5" Howitzers assisted by the Heavy Artillery.
The operation will be in 3 phases.

Phase 1. Howitzers bombard mortars for 5', after the Howitzers have been shooting 2' the 18-prs form the barrage and shoot for 3'.

Phase 2. All guns and Howitzers cease firing.

Phase 3. Phase 1. repeated.

DETAIL.
3. O.C. St. Eloi Group will detail batteries to destroy CUPID in accordance with attached schedule A.
O.C. DIEPENDAAL Group will detail batteries to destroy FREDERICK in accordance with attached schedule B.
FREDERICK's pin point as verified by the latest air photographs is N.18.b.9½.3½.

HEAVY ARTILLERY. The Heavy Artillery will be asked to co-operate.

RATES OF FIRE. AMMUNITION. Rates of fire and allotment of ammunition will be as laid down in schedule A & B.

PREPARATION. O.C Groups will make all arrangements at once for carrying out this operation.

ZERO HOUR Watches will be synchronised with this office at 9 a.m. on November 29th Zero Hour will be 11.30 a.m.

8. ACKNOWLEDGE.

H Hulton
Brigade Major
41st Divisional Arty.

Copy No. 1 War Diary
" " 2 FILE.
" " 3 St. Eloi Group
         6
" " 7 DIEPENDAAL Group
         10
" " 11 187th Bde.
" " 12 41st Divsn G
" " 13   Q
" " 14 10th Corps H.A.
" " 15 10th
" " 16 Belgians 7th Gp.

SCHEDULE "A"

Guns	Period	TASK	Co-ordinates	rds per gun per min	AX	BX	Total
(a) 3 18-pr	2' after Z to 5' after Z	Barrage	O.8.a.6.7.48-O.8.a.78.48	1	9		9
(b) 3 "	"	"	O.8.a.78.48 - O.8.a.78.35	1	9		9
(c) 3 "	"	"	O.8.a.78.35 - O.8.a.67.38	1	9		9
(d) 3 "	"	"	O.8.a.67.38 - O.8.a.67.48	1	9		9
(e) 6 4.5" Hows	Z to 5' after Z	Bombard	O.8.a.7.4.	1		30	30
(f) 3 18-pr	12' after Z to 15' after Z	Barrage	(as in (a))	1	9		9
(g) 3 "	"	"	" (b)	1	9		9
(h) 3 "	"	"	" (c)	1	9		9
(i) 3 "	"	"	" (d)	1	9		9
(j) 6 4.5" Hows	10' after Z to 15' after Z	Bombard	" (e)	1		30	30
					72	60	132
			From Schedule B		72	60	132
			GRAND TOTAL		144	120	264

SCHEDULE B

Guns	Period	Task	Co-ordinates	rds per gun per min.	4X	3X	Total
(k) 3 18-prs	2' after Z to 5' after Z	Barrage	N.18.b.97.45 - O.13.a.02.36	1	9		9
(l) 3 18-prs	"	"	O.13.a.02.36 N.18.b.95.30	1	9		9
(m) 3 18-prs	"	"	N.18.b.95.30 - N.18.b.89.37	1	9		9
(n) 3 18-prs	"	"	N.18.b.89.37 - N.18.b.97.45	1	9		9
(o) 6 4.5"How	Z to 5' after Z	Bombard	N.18.b.9½.3½	1		30	30
(p) 3 18-prs	12' after Z to 15' after Z	Barrage	as in (k)	1	9		9
(q) 3 18-prs	"	"	as in (l)	1	9		9
(r) 3 18-prs	"	"	as in (m)	1	9		9
(s) 3 18-prs	"	"	as in (n)	1	9		9
(t) 6 4.5"How	10' after Z to 15' after Z	Bombard	as in (o)	1		30	30
					72	60	132

189th Bde R.F.A.

Army Form C. 2118.

DECEMBER
PAGE 1.

Vol 8

WAR DIARY
or
INTELLIGENCE SUMMARY.
(Erase heading not required.)

Place	Date	Hour	Summary of Events and Information	Remarks and references to Appendices
H.Q. 500 yds N.E. of DICKEBUSCHE	1st.		Ordinary troops. Quiet day.	Very cold + frosty
"	2nd.		Headquarters relieved by 187 Bde. Headquarters and hosted at 187 Bde Headquarters 400 yds North of DICKEBUSCHE. C and D Batteries Reft to DIEPENDAAL GROUP for 41st DA order No 39.	fine
H.Q. 400 yds N of DICKEBUSCHE	3rd.		C + D Batteries retired to rest at their wagon lines. B battery still in action under ST. ELOI GROUP.	fine
"	4th.		Old D/189 (Capt. G.W. HART) reorganised into a gun battery and becomes D/189. (Capt JENKINS) D/189 Renamed D/190. D/190 (Capt. LEVENTHORPE) becomes A/189 and remains in action. H.Q. and C Battery at rest.	
"	5th.		"	
"	6th.		"	
"	7th.		D/189 Relieved by D/190, and retired to rest in Wagon lines H.Q. and C + D Batteries at rest.	wet
"	8th.		"	fine
"	9th.		"	fine
"	10th.		"	

Army Form C. 2118.

WAR DIARY
or
INTELLIGENCE SUMMARY.
(Erase heading not required.)

DECEMBER PAGE 2

Place	Date	Hour	Summary of Events and Information	Remarks and references to Appendices
H.Q. 400 yds N. of DICKEBUSCHE HK			H.Q. and C and D Batteries at rest.	
"	12th		"	fine wet.
"	13th		"	fine misty
"	14th		"	fine "
"	15th		B/189 returned to rest	
"	16th		at their wagon lines	fine misty
"	17th		H.Q. meeting. B, C & D Batteries at rest at wagon lines.	fine "
"	18th		"	fine misty
"	19th		"	snow
"	20th		"	fine frosty
"	21st		"	wet
"	22		"	wet
"	23		"	Heavy gale
"	24		"	Very heavy gale
"	25		"	with rainfall

Army Form C. 2118.

WAR DIARY
or
INTELLIGENCE SUMMARY.
(Erase heading not required.)

DECEMBER PAGE III

Place	Date	Hour	Summary of Events and Information	Remarks and references to Appendices
H.Q. HOOGE N. & DICKEBUSCHE	Dec. 26		H.Q. B, C, & D batteries at rest in wagon lines. Nothing to Report.	
"	27		" " " " " "	
"	28		" " " " " "	
"	29		" " " " " "	
"	30		" " " " " "	
"	31		" " " " " "	

W McCue
Lieut-Col. R.F.A.
Comdg. 189 Brigade R.F.A.

WAR DIARY
or
INTELLIGENCE SUMMARY.

JANUARY 1917

R.A. 18 of the R.X. PAGE I.

A/189

Place	Date	Hour	Summary of Events and Information	Remarks and references to Appendices
H.Q. 500 yards N of DICKEBUSCH	1.		Headquarters, B, C and D batteries in rest.	Showery fine
	2.		"	"
	3.		"	"
	4.		"	"
	5.		"	"
	6.		"	"
	7.		"	"
	8.		"	"
	9.		A/189 becomes D/190. H.Q. B C and D Batteries in rest. 2, 4, 5 Howitzers of D/189 left to DIEPENDAAL GROUP for 41st D.A. Operation Order No. A9.	
	10.		One Section B/189 relieved One Section {3/190} in the DIEPENDAAL A/190 SECTOR.	Cold. Slight snow
	11.		" A C/189 " " " " "	rain & snow

Army Form C. 2118.

WAR DIARY
or
INTELLIGENCE SUMMARY.
(Erase heading not required.)

JAN 1917 PAGE 2

Place	Date	Hour	Summary of Events and Information	Remarks and references to Appendices
H.Q. 500 yds N. of DICKEBUSCHE	JAN 12		One section B/189 relieved one section B/190 } in the DIEPENDAAL " " C/189 " " " A/190 } SECTOR. 4.5" Howitzers of D/189 lent to RIGHT GROUP, 23rd Divl. ARTY. per 41st D.A. O.O. No. 49.	Wet
HQ at LA CLYTTE	13.		Headquarters 190 Bde RFA in DIEPENDAAL SECTOR.	Cold Wet.
	14.		Quiet. D/190 registered for 41st O.O. No 52. by aeroplane	Frosty, foggy
	15.		Quiet dy.	some snow frost, fog. N.O.R. accidentally killed
	16. 7.15am		D/190 carried out 41st DA O.O. No 52. Wire cut by M.T.M. No. 07a and 0.7.C. (41st DA O.O. No 51) Bearing fire provided by B/189, C/190 and D/190. D/189 returned to the wagon lines	Some snow & frost.
	17.		Quiet day.	
	18. 3.30pm		Wire cut by French Mortar, Bearing fire provided	
	19.		Quiet day. 11.30pm. 41st. D.A.O.O. No51 carried out.	
	20.		One section C/236 joined D/189, & relieved one section of D/190 One section 34th Battery RFA relieved one section C/190	LT. S.C. WILLIAMS KILLED. 2 O.Rs. Accidentally Killed

Army Form C. 2118.

WAR DIARY
or
INTELLIGENCE SUMMARY.
(Erase heading not required.)

JAN. 1917
PAGE 3.

Instructions regarding War Diaries and Intelligence Summaries are contained in F.S. Regs., Part II. and the Staff Manual respectively. Title pages will be prepared in manuscript.

Place	Date	Hour	Summary of Events and Information	Remarks and references to Appendices
H.Q at LACLYTTE	21.		D/189 relieved D/190. 34th Battery joined this Brigade and relieved C/190.	
	22.		Quiet day.	Colo. Hull, Fine, Colo.
	23.		"	"
	24.		"	"
	25.		"	"
	26.		"	"
	27.		"	"
	28.		"	"
	29.		"	"
	30.		BOIS QUARANTE bombarded by D/189. Group shoot on ONRAET FARM.	1 O.R. wounded. 1 O.R. wounded.
	31		B/189 calibrating. Quiet Day.	

Mus Lane
Major R.F.A
o/c 189 Brigade R.F.A

189 Bde R.F.A.
Vol 10

Army Form C. 2118.

WAR DIARY
or
INTELLIGENCE SUMMARY.
(Erase heading not required.)

Place	Date	Hour	Summary of Events and Information	Remarks and references to Appendices
La Clyte	13th		Batteries pulled out in expectation of the relief. 187" Batteries take their places.	
La Clyte Dickebusch	14th		Howsers on Dickebusch Group to 190 B.D. took over Gt Eloi group from 187 B.D.	
"	15th		Batteries took over from 187 B.D. in St Eloi group. Quiet day.	
"	16th		Very misty all day and registration impossible. All quiet.	
"	17th		Enemy action with T.M.s & 10.5 cm on our front line. Retaliation. Misty day.	
"	18th		18/prs registers on 47th Div front to 00.59. Casualties 22824 Gr Ayre, 130429 Gr Woodward 1111351 Gr HaiSacre, Gr Hempsey all hurt in accident to cookhouse. 5 Tel lines changed. D/189	
"	19th		Misty day with poor observation. Quiet. Brig. Gen. Potter RFA hands over group to Lt Col Symonds. Leaves for 34th Div. as C.R.A.	

Army Form C. 2118.

WAR DIARY
or
INTELLIGENCE SUMMARY.
(Erase heading not required.)

Instructions regarding War Diaries and Intelligence Summaries are contained in F. S. Regs., Part II. and the Staff Manual respectively. Title pages will be prepared in manuscript.

Place	Date	Hour	Summary of Events and Information	Remarks and references to Appendices
"	20		O.O. 59 Carried out according to programme, as ordered.	
"	21		Very quiet day. Misty & observation poor. Position preparation in progress.	Raining
"	22		Quiet day. Very misty. Preparation of front/enemy position. C/104 & C/236 active at night.	
"	23		Cove cutting into T.M.S & 18 pdrs. Centuries on craters. Preliminary Bombardment to O.O. 60. Very misty.	
"	24		O.O. N° 60 carried out as ordered. Col. Eardly Wilmot injured to take over Group. Misty weather. Raid by 10th Queens successful. Prisoners captured. One Gen. wounded.	
"	25		Quiet day. C/104 + C/236 leave this area.	
"	26		Hostile artillery somewhat active. Fine day.	
"	27		Quiet day. Col. Eardly Wilmot taken over command of Group.	
Dickebusch	28/1/17		Quiet day. Etcom: Amount of Trench Mortar activity.	

Lieut-Col R.F.A
Commanding ..... Brigade R.F.A

189 Bde RFA
MAR. PAGE 1.

Army Form C. 2118.

WAR DIARY
or
INTELLIGENCE SUMMARY.
(Erase heading not required.)

Vol XI
MAR. PAGE I.

Place	Date	Hour	Summary of Events and Information	Remarks and references to Appendices
H.Q. 500 yds NE of DICKEBUSCHE	MAR. 1.	12.30pm	C/189 detached section and D/189 detached section shelled for four hours. 2 LT. W.O.H. JOYNSON wounded. MAJOR R.H.A.D. LOVE wounded (still at duty), LT. D. PAGE THOMAS wounded. 1 O.R. wounded 1 O.R. killed.	Fine day.
"	2		Quiet day. Fired on Enemy roads throughout night on account of reported relief.	Fine day.
"	3		" " " "	"
"	4		" " " " Dispersed three working parties.	Fine day.
"	5	8.30am	Dispersed working party. Quiet day.	Visibility very poor.
"	6.	9.30am	" " "	Fine.
"		3PM.	Trench Mortars cut wire at O8 a 3.8. Evening fire provided.	
"	7.	6.30am	P.B. shoot as ordered by A/104 & D/189. Trench mortars cut wire at O8 a 3.8. Covering fire provided.	Fine. Strong north wind.
"	8		Trench mortars cut wire. Evening fire provided.	Fine. Observation good. Road short.
"	9		Hostile artillery active, batteries retaliated. Road shoot.	Fine, visibility good.
"	10		Road shoot in evening. Trench mortar shoot with covering fire.	Observation good.
"	11		Quiet day — nothing to report.	
"	12.		Trench mortars cut wire, covering fire provided.	Observation good.

Army Form C. 2118.

WAR DIARY
or
INTELLIGENCE SUMMARY.
(Erase heading not required.)

MAR page 2

Place	Date	Hour	Summary of Events and Information	Remarks and references to Appendices
Dickebusch	13th		Trench mortars cut wire & batteries provide covering fire.	
"	14th		OO.6.2. 41st D.A. East survey attempt carried out. (curtailed). The party was under Klaw on trenches. Barrage reported good.	
"	15th		Enemy shelling heavy. Half batteries relieved by 187 B.D. Casualties, Major Hart killed. Capt. Johnson killed. 2nd Lt. D/189.	
"	16		Batteries complete relief. Command of 21 Cdn: Group taken over by OC 187 B⁴.	
Hondschoote	17th		Brigade arrived in Watou / Houtkerque areas less 34th Battery in action.	
"	18th		Brigade in rest.	
Rivelet	19th		Brigade moves to Rivelet area.	
"	20		Rest in above area.	
Noordpeene	21st		Brigade marched to Noordpeene.	
Muicque Nieurlet	22		" to Polincove area. (H.Q. at Muicque Nieurlet.)	
"	23		Brigade in rest at above.	
"	24		" " "	
"	25		" " "	
"	26		" " " 34th Battery join 187 Bd at La Panne.	

Army Form C. 2118.

WAR DIARY
or
INTELLIGENCE SUMMARY.
(Erase heading not required.)

MAR Page 3

Place	Date	Hour	Summary of Events and Information	Remarks and references to Appendices
Mucque Nieulet	27th		B⁹ in rest as above.	
"	28th		" " " "	
"	29th		" " " "	
"	30th		" " " "	
"	31st		" " " "	

F.J. Taylor
for............Lieut-Col. R.F.A.
Comdg. 189 Brigade R.F.A.

WAR DIARY or INTELLIGENCE SUMMARY.

Army Form C. 2118.

189 Bde R[FA]
APRIL PAGE 1
Vol 12

Place	Date	Hour	Summary of Events and Information	Remarks and references to Appendices
MONCQ NIEURLET.	1		Brigade in Rest.	
"	2		" " "	
"	3		B/189 moved in to action near DICKEBUSCHE. YPRES.	
"	4		16/189 " " " " "	
"	4th		Remainder of Brigade at Rest.	
"	5th		" " " "	
"	6th		" " " "	
"	7th		" " " "	
Noordpeene	8th		Left Moncq Nieurlet. vanins at Noordpeene.	
Recuisfeld	9th		Bde H.Q. + D/189 arrive at 41st Div area, also C Battery from 47th Div area.	
"	10th		38th Brigade HQ. at trouts near HOSTELE.	
"	11th		B38. Coss 34th Battery MBAC in wagon line reserve.	
"	12th		Brigade in wagon line reserve. work on new positions etc.	
"	13th		" " " " " " "	
"	14th		" " " " " " "	
"	15th		" " " " " " "	

Army Form C. 2118.

WAR DIARY
or
INTELLIGENCE SUMMARY.
(Erase heading not required.)

Instructions regarding War Diaries and Intelligence Summaries are contained in F. S. Regs., Part II. and the Staff Manual respectively. Title pages will be prepared in manuscript.

Place	Date	Hour	Summary of Events and Information	Remarks and references to Appendices
RANINGHELST	16th		Work on positions by Batteries.	
"	17th		"	
"	18th		Working parties from B/A.C. & 34th Batteries arrive. Lt. Col. Grenadge takes command of 88.	
"	19th		One section of B, C, & D Batteries go into action at YPRES.	
YPRES	20th		HQ and remaining sections of B, C & D Batteries go into action at YPRES. Relief completed without casualties. Group consists of B.C. & D/189, B/104, D/189. 1 sec A/103, 1 sec D/104	
YPRES	21st		Registration by Batteries.	
YPRES	22nd		Registration by Batteries; orders for B/104 & D/189 test wire.	
YPRES	23rd		Heavy Arty Bombard Hill 60. B/104 shelled in evening	
YPRES	24th		2nd day of Bombardment by Heavy Arty. B/104 cuts wire. Orders arrive for G.A. scheme	
"	25th		Hostile artillery quieter. Nothing to report.	

Army Form C. 2118.

WAR DIARY
or
INTELLIGENCE SUMMARY.
(Erase heading not required.)

Instructions regarding War Diaries and Intelligence Summaries are contained in F. S. Regs., Part II. and the Staff Manual respectively. Title pages will be prepared in manuscript.

Place	Date	Hour	Summary of Events and Information	Remarks and references to Appendices
YPRES	26		B/104 continue wire cutting.	
"	27		Lt. Col. Thorntons assumed command of 118th Bde vice Lt. Col. Grundy. B/104 cut wire. Hostile artillery quiet.	
"	28		Hostile artillery quiet. Nothing to report.	
"	29		Orders given to B.Cs. re 24 special points for notice. Raid on left Divr front.	
YPRES	30/5		Received orders for possible attack on HILL 60. One OR wounded returned to duty. Court Martial on Gr. J.A. Harris B/Battery. Battery registration of new points.	

J. Allen Lt Col.
RFA
29/5/15

www.ingramcontent.com/pod-product-compliance
Lightning Source LLC
Chambersburg PA
CBHW081241170426
43191CB00034B/2001